Juliette Clarke
1990

OTHER BOOKS IN THIS SERIES:
For a wonderful Mother A book to make your own
For a wonderful Grandmother A book to make your own
A Girl's Journal A personal notebook and keepsake
A Woman's Journal A personal notebook and keepsake
Cats A book to make your own
Teddy Bears A book to make your own
Inspirations A book to make your own
A Gardener's Journal A book to make your own
OTHER HELEN EXLEY GIFTBOOKS
FOR FRIENDS:
The Love Between Friends
Thank Heavens for Friends
To a very special Friend
A Little Book for a Friend

Published in hardback 1990. Published in softcover 2001.
Copyright © Helen Exley 1990, 2001
Selection © Helen Exley 1990, 2001
The moral right of the author has been asserted.

12 11 10 9 8 7 6

ISBN 1-86187-213-5

Selection and design by Helen Exley
Illustrated by Juliette Clarke
Printed in China

Helen Exley Giftbooks, 16 Chalk Hill, Watford, Herts, WD19 4BG, UK.
Helen Exley Giftbooks LLC, 185 Main Street, Spencer, MA 01562, USA.
www.helenexleygiftbooks.com.

For a real
Friend

A BOOK TO
MAKE YOUR OWN

A HELEN EXLEY GIFTBOOK

⊟EXLEY

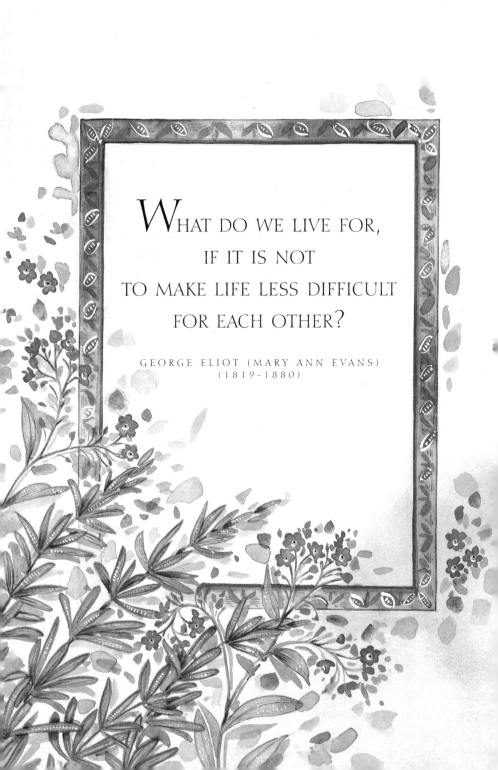

WHAT DO WE LIVE FOR,
IF IT IS NOT
TO MAKE LIFE LESS DIFFICULT
FOR EACH OTHER?

GEORGE ELIOT (MARY ANN EVANS)
(1819-1880)

$\mathcal{Y}$es, there is a talkability
that can express itself even without words.
There is an exchange of thought and feeling
which is happy alike in speech and in silence.
It is quietness pervaded with friendship.

HENRY VAN DYKE

*Friendship, although incredibly sensitive to mood and need,
is apparently blind to appearances.
Schoolfriends – skinny, spotty, besotted with ballet and palominos –
see no change in each other, forty years on.*

PAM BROWN, B.1928

WHOEVER
IS HAPPY
WILL MAKE OTHERS
HAPPY TOO.

ANNE FRANK (1929-1945)

Juliette Clarke

THAT BEST PORTION OF A GOOD MAN'S LIFE,
HIS LITTLE, NAMELESS,
UNREMEMBERED ACTS OF KINDNESS AND OF LOVE.

WILLIAM WORDSWORTH (1770-1850)

*Friendship is always a sweet
responsibility, never an opportunity.*

KAHLIL GIBRAN (1883-1931)

$\mathcal{T}$here's nothing worth the wear of winning,
but laughter and the love of friends.

HILAIRE BELLOC (1870-1953)

THE TEST OF FRIENDSHIP
IS ASSISTANCE IN
ADVERSITY, AND THAT,
TOO, UNCONDITIONAL
ASSISTANCE.

MAHATMA GANDHI
(1869-1948)

The thread of our life would be dark, Heaven knows!
If it were not with friendship and love intertwin'd.

THOMAS MOORE (1779-1852)

Friendships link and loop and interweave until they mesh the world.

PAM BROWN, B.1928

FRIENDS, BOOKS,
A CHEERFUL HEART, AND
CONSCIENCE CLEAR
ARE THE MOST
CHOICE COMPANIONS
WE HAVE HERE.

WILLIAM MATHER

*What a wretched lot
of old shrivelled creatures
we shall be by-and-by.
Never mind — the uglier
we get in the eyes of others,
the lovelier we shall be
to each other.*

GEORGE ELIOT (MARY ANN EVANS)
(1819-1880)

*The best rule of friendship
is to keep your heart
a little softer
than your head.*

GEORGE SANTAYANA (1863-1952)

A FRIEND IS A PRESENT
WHICH YOU GIVE YOURSELF.

ROBERT LOUIS STEVENSON (1850-1894)

HOLD A TRUE FRIEND
WITH BOTH YOUR HANDS.

NIGERIAN PROVERB

I love you not only for what you are,
but for what I am when I am with you.
I love you not only for what you have made
of yourself, but for what you are making of me.

ROY CROFT

My
BEST FRIEND
IS THE ONE
WHO BRINGS OUT
THE BEST IN ME.

HENRY FORD

$\mathscr{A}$ FRIEND MAY WELL BE RECKONED

THE MASTERPIECE OF NATURE.

RALPH WALDO EMERSON (1803-1882)

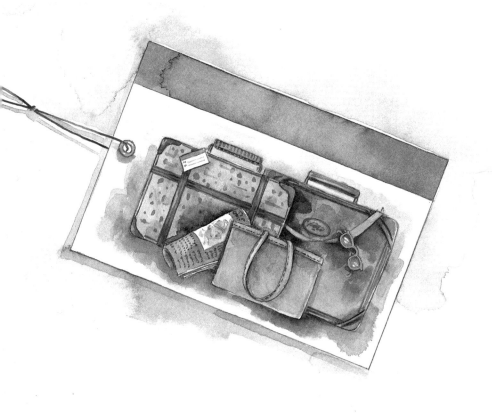

Each friend represents a world in us,
a world possibly not born until they arrive,
and it is only by this meeting that a new world is born.

ANAÏS NIN (1903-1977)

A little more kindness, a little less creed,
A little more giving, a little less greed,
A little more smile, a little less frown,
A little less kicking a man when he's down,
A little more "we", and a little less "I",
A little more laugh, a little less cry,
A little more flowers on the pathway of life,
And fewer on graves at the end of the strife.

ANONYMOUS

$\mathcal{D}$o not keep the alabaster boxes of your love and tenderness sealed up until your friends are dead. Fill their lives with sweetness. Speak approving cheering words while their ears can hear them and while their hearts can be thrilled by them.

GEORGE W. CHILDS

Our different homes perhaps a continent apart.
All my dear friends. Known only for a brief time
and sometimes so long ago,
but alive forever in my mind and heart.

HELEN THOMSON, B.1943

*W*ishing to be friends is quick work,
but friendship is a slow-ripening fruit.

ARISTOTLE (384-322 B.C.)

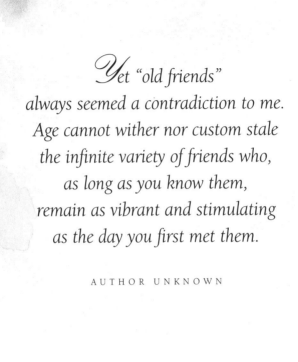

Yet "old friends"
always seemed a contradiction to me.
Age cannot wither nor custom stale
the infinite variety of friends who,
as long as you know them,
remain as vibrant and stimulating
as the day you first met them.

AUTHOR UNKNOWN

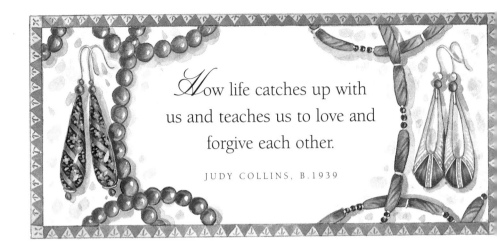

How life catches up with
us and teaches us to love and
forgive each other.

JUDY COLLINS, B.1939

I<small>F I CAN STOP ONE HEART</small>
<small>FROM BREAKING,</small>
I <small>SHALL NOT LIVE IN VAIN;</small>
I<small>F I CAN EASE ONE LIFE</small>
<small>THE ACHING,</small>
O<small>R COOL ONE PAIN</small>
O<small>R HELP ONE FAINTING ROBIN</small>
U<small>NTO HIS NEST AGAIN,</small>
I <small>SHALL NOT LIVE IN VAIN.</small>

EMILY DICKINSON
(1830-1886)

$\mathscr{Y}$ou can't fake listening.
It shows.

RAQUEL WELCH, B.1942

*M*oney can buy many things,
good and evil.
All the wealth of the world
could not buy you a friend
or pay you for the loss of one.

G . D . P R E N T I C E

WISE SAYINGS OFTEN FALL ON BARREN GROUND;
BUT A KIND WORD IS NEVER THROWN AWAY.

SIR ARTHUR HELPS (1813-1875)

$\mathcal{F}$riendship is unnecessary,
like philosophy, like art.... It has no
survival value; rather it is one of those
things that give value to survival.

C.S. LEWIS (1898-1963)

*O*ld friends are best.
King James used to call for his old shoes;
they were easiest for his feet.

JOHN SELDON (1584-1654)

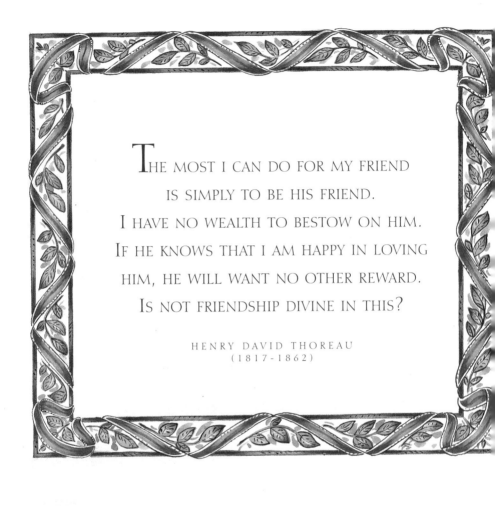

THE MOST I CAN DO FOR MY FRIEND
IS SIMPLY TO BE HIS FRIEND.
I HAVE NO WEALTH TO BESTOW ON HIM.
IF HE KNOWS THAT I AM HAPPY IN LOVING
HIM, HE WILL WANT NO OTHER REWARD.
IS NOT FRIENDSHIP DIVINE IN THIS?

HENRY DAVID THOREAU
(1817-1862)

*E*ffua put her hand on my cheek:
"Sister, you have need of a sister-friend because you need to
weep and you need someone to watch you while you weep".

MAYA ANGELOU, B.1928

True happiness consists not in the multitude of friends,
But in the worth and choice.

BEN JONSON (1572-1637)

For whoever knows how to return a kindness he has received
must be a friend above all price.

SOPHOCLES (469-406 B.C.)

IT IS VERY EASY TO FORGIVE
OTHERS THEIR MISTAKES;
IT TAKES MORE GRIT AND GUMPTION TO FORGIVE THEM
FOR HAVING WITNESSED YOUR OWN.

JESSAMYN WEST, B.1902

Happiness seems made to be shared.

JEAN RACINE (1639-1699)

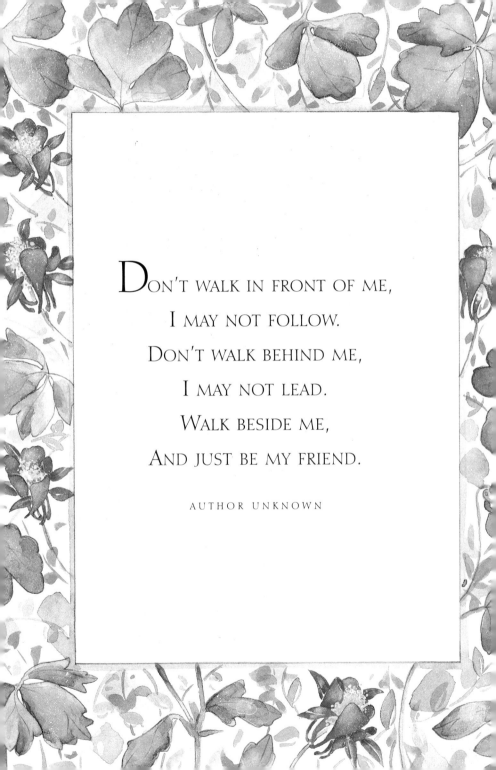

Don't walk in front of me,
I may not follow.
Don't walk behind me,
I may not lead.
Walk beside me,
And just be my friend.

AUTHOR UNKNOWN

*I no doubt deserved
my enemies,
but I don't believe
I deserved my friends.*

WALT WHITMAN
(1819-1892)

Juliette Clarke
1990